MW01121396

160201

L E O

LEO

Rosa Laborde

Playwrights Canada Press
Toronto • Canada

Playwrights Canada Press
The Canadian Drama Publisher
215 Spadina Ave., Suite 230, Toronto, Ontario CANADA M5T 2C7
416.703.0013   fax 416.408.3402
orders@playwrightscanada.com • www.playwrightscanada.com

Financial support provided by the taxpayers of Canada and Ontario through the
Canada Council for the Arts and the Department of Canadian Heritage through the
Book Publishing Industry Development Programme, and the Ontario Arts Council.

Front cover image Prey Reversal. Oil and collage on canvas, 56″ x 56″, 1998.
www.tamaratoledo.com
Cover design: JLArt
Production Editor: MZK

Library and Archives Canada Cataloguing in Publication

Laborde, Rosa

Leo / Rosa Laborde.

A play.

ISBN 0-88754-898-9

I. Title.

PS8623.A264L46 2006   C812'.6   C2006-903574-1

First edition: November 2006.
Printed and bound by Canadian Printco at Scarborough, Canada.

• Dedication •

This play is for:

My mother and grandmother, both named Léo, who have spent a lifetime outside of the country they call home because they dared to stand for what they believed in.

For the members of my family who still believe the coup was the best thing that could have happened to Chile.

For everyone left behind to mend the pieces of a country's broken spirit.

For the disappeared.

•Introduction•

Discussions about *Leo* inevitably evolve to the crucial issue of time and place. "Is it set the night Leo was interrogated/tortured by the Chilean army?" "Does the play start as a reflection after he has died or as he was dying (the last flash through the memories of an all too brief life)?" "I don't understand, where in hell is the play supposed to be set?" "It makes no sense." Rosa's struggle to define the "where and when" in her play was palpable. Throughout her development process, she kept revisiting, re-writing the outward frame of the play—an emerging playwright attempting to land the play in a place that stayed true to her instincts and yet would be comprehended. Rosa's final decision was her first decision. Returning to her original impulse: she set the play in a time and space we cannot know—in the space and time of the *desaparecidos*— the disappeared.

The world of the disappeared is a world created of grasping comprehension. It is the world of those of us left behind—the survivors, the un-arrested, the released, the escapees, the passive observers, and the innocent bystanders. We can only understand the time and place of the disappeared as an absence that has no end of space and no finite time. The time of the disappeared is endless, their home a place always seeking definition but can never be known. Where is the play set? It is set in a place we cannot know except by the longing of those of us left behind who have no definition about the whereabouts and circumstances of loved ones disappeared.

In setting the play in the homeland of the disappeared, *Leo* is a remarkable but painful experience evidenced by the nightly weeping in the audience. The play captures the sub-conscious of a country where the disappearance of loved ones was a premeditated act of psychological terror by the army and government. This particular and individual suffering (not knowing whether husbands, sons, wives and daughters have died or not) became part of a nation's conscience and identity—an emblem of nationality. Rosa captures the people and a country to this day recovering from the trauma of a military coup. While these circumstances are distinct of Chile, the notion of loved ones disappeared is visceral, relatable and imaginable even to those audience members who know nothing of Chile's history.

For those of you who go on to direct, design, act or simply read this play, it is a play that will ask you to imagine the unknowable, to believe in a world you cannot define by the corners of space and finite time and to create a world that is more feeling than actual, more palpable than tangible, more longing than knowable. *Leo* is a good play because it asks of artist and audience alike to imagine to the limits of imagination much like every parent or lover or family member who has lost a loved one to the *desaparecidos*.

Richard Rose
Artistic Director
Tarragon Theatre

• Acknowledgements •

Thank you to: Leonor Rosas, Leonor Leon Laborde, Costanza Duran, Marcelo Puente, Salvatore Antonio, The Salvador Allende Arts Festival For Peace, Richard Rose, Andy McKim, Mark Lockington, Melissa-Jane Shaw, Clare Giuliani, Justin Roddy, The Rhubarb! Festival and Buddies In Bad Times Theatre, Naomi Campbell, Ian Carpenter, Devi, Susan & David, Nisa & Matthew, Micheline Chevrier, Absit Omen, Rick Roberts, Jennifer Tarver, Nicole Stamp, Kate Hennig, David Macfarlane and, of course, my dad.

With love and gratitude for two angels of the theatre: Bruce Vavrina & Paul Bettis. You left too soon.

•Playwright's Notes•

I have always been obsessed with the circumstances of my birth.

In 1973 the political coup in Chile sent a politically active seventeen-year-old Chilean girl reeling into culture shock in North America, her feet finally hitting the ground in Ottawa, Ontario where she met my father, and out I came in 1978.

So I am Canadian; born in our nation's capital a stone's throw from our parliament buildings, a breath away from our National Art Gallery.

But I am also Chilean. In my hips. In my heart. In my temper. Had the tragedy of the *coup d'état* never happened I would not exist. Spanish words were the first to touch my tongue, Chile was the mythical country we were supposed to live in, Salvador Allende was nothing short of God.

Being socially aware was a given in my family, wanting to make a difference, needing to see the world become a better place. These qualities are a part of my fascia, the connective tissue holding the structure of who I am together.

But I am also a hedonist; a lover of good wine and food, sex and pleasure, shiny new shoes and plush surroundings.

It is at the centre of this struggle that *Leo* was born.

• • •

Leo is pronounced with Spanish accent — \layo\.

l to r: Cara Pifko, Salvatore Antonio, Sergio Di Zio
photo by Cylla von Tiedemann

Leo premiered at the Tarragon Theatre, Toronto, in February 2006, with the following company:

LEO   Salvatore Antonio
RODRIGO   Sergio Di Zio
ISOLDA   Cara Pifko
VOICE OF MAMI   Francisca Zentilli

Directed by Richard Rose
Music Composed and Performed by Marcelo Puente
Set and Lighting Design by Graeme S. Thomson
Costumes Coordinated by Jolene Antle
Sound Design by Thomas Ryder Payne

• • •

Leo was first presented as a short piece in The Rhubarb! Festival at Buddies in Bad Times Theatre with the following actors: Salvatore Antonio, Andy Velasquez, Elana McMurtry and has been since workshopped through Tarragon Theatre's Playwright's Unit with: Marcello Cabezas, Darrell Dennis, Cara Pifko, Noam Jenkins, Marilo Nunez, Sergio Di Zio and Kathryn Winslow.

•Characters•

Leo
Rodrigo
Isolda
Mami

> *The stage is bare but for a plain wooden chair.*
> *A naked lightbulb hangs down over it. LEO sits in*
> *the chair. The lightbulb casts shadows across his face.*
> *He smokes.*

LEO   *Absolutismo, autoritarismo, colectivismo, comunismo,*
democracia, humo, fascismo, federalismo, (accent)
imperialism, liberalism, smoke, *(normal)*
nationalism, socialism, smoke, totalitarianism,
Utopianism... smoke, smoke, smoke! Theories,
doctrines, principles, bullshit! Words to live by.
Words to fight for. Words to kill for.

> *He is hit in the face. A breath breaks out of his body.*
> *A smoky haze slowly begins to fill the space. The*
> *sound of water rises. It has become difficult for LEO*
> *to breathe.*

And the current... dragging you down... the
whirlpool the whirlpool... like the universe knows
we're entering into a darker place... there is nothing
left to see... my feet, my fingers, my blood... and
nothing? If there is nothing. If I see nothing. If
nothing sees me...

> *Lights begin to fade.*

To cease to be seen. To vanish from sight. To cease to
exist or be known.

> *Lights snap to black.*

No!!!

> *Sounds of candy hitting the floor. Lights come up on*
> *LEO wearing a blindfold. Candy is strewn on the*
> *floor in front of him. It is a backyard birthday party.*
> *They are children.*

MAMI   *Abre los ojos mi hijo.*

RODRIGO   Open your eyes, Leo.

ISOLDA   Yeah. Open your eyes.

> *LEO takes off his blindfold and looks down at all of the candy. ISOLDA, RODRIGO & MAMI sing "Feliz Cumpleanos" ["Happy Birthday"].*

ISOLDA,
RODRIGO
& MAMI   *Feliz cumpleanos a ti...*

> *LEO joins in the song. They all sing together.*

LEO   *Feliz cumpleanos a mi.... Feliz cumpleanos a Leonardo Francisco Rosas Mella.... Feliz cumpleanos a mi.*

> *He drops to the floor and begins collecting his candy.*

ISOLDA   May I have a piece of candy?

LEO   No.

ISOLDA   But—

LEO   No.

RODRIGO   One candy for everyone. It's only fair.

LEO   No.

RODRIGO   Yes.

LEO   But it's my birthday.

RODRIGO   I'm leaving, Leo, if you don't share.

> *LEO panics. Remembering what hasn't happened yet.*

LEO   No, Rodrigo, just follow me. Please *hombre*.

> *Back to party.*

ISOLDA   Puhlease!

> *LEO hands ISOLDA one candy only. She steals two more without him seeing.*

Thank you, Leo.

> *She kisses him on his cheek. He likes it. He gives her another candy, waits for her to kiss him. She doesn't.*

LEO	*Dame un beso.*
	She does. LEO decides to hand candy out to everyone else at his party (audience members) while humming "Happy Birthday" to himself and requesting kisses for each candy he gives. He does this three times. When he gets to the third person he asks them to kiss him three times. He could seemingly go on forever. A glass smashes.
	Mami!
RODRIGO	Leo, I'm sorry.
LEO	What?
RODRIGO	Well. Your father.
LEO	Uh huh.
RODRIGO	It's really hard when people…
LEO	Leave.
RODRIGO	Yeah. Leave.
ISOLDA	I'm done with my father so… if you want him…?
LEO	Parents aren't like children, Soli, you can't just give them away.
ISOLDA	Shame.
LEO	Yeah.
RODRIGO	So we'll do a ceremony I thought—like an offering —we'll dig a hole in the ground.
ISOLDA	I brought candy.
RODRIGO	Good. There are four candies, so we can each have one and then one for the hole.
LEO	Does the hole really need a candy?
RODRIGO	It's part of the offering.
LEO	It's a waste of a good candy.

RODRIGO   What do you propose?

LEO   I will have that candy.

RODRIGO   If you have that candy, we'll have had one and you'll have had two and it won't be fair.

LEO   Better we should be fair to the hole?

ISOLDA   Now what?

RODRIGO   We bury our deepest secret.

ISOLDA   Why.

RODRIGO   Because that's the plan.

ISOLDA   Because why.

RODRIGO   Our secrets will grow into the ground like roots and we'll be part of Chile forever.

LEO   I don't want to play anymore.

ISOLDA   My father sleeps with my nanny. That's my secret.

> *She spits in the hole and buries it.*

How's that for roots?

> *Awkward pause as the boys look at her.*

RODRIGO   Uh... Leo?

LEO   Yeah?

RODRIGO   Your turn.

LEO   My father disappeared in the Bermuda Triangle.

> *The game has not gone as RODRIGO planned.*

RODRIGO   Okay...

LEO   He went to fight in the revolution with Che.

ISOLDA   Guevara?

LEO   But things got bad so he escaped on a freighter. A freighter that disappeared in the Bermuda Triangle. No one knows about it.

ISOLDA   If no one knows then how do you know?

RODRIGO   Soli.

ISOLDA   Oh. Good secret.

RODRIGO   Now bury it.

> *LEO spits on the ground and begins to cover his secret.*

MAMI   *Donde estas Leo?*

LEO   I'm right here, Mami. Can you see me?

MAMI   *No, Leo.*

LEO   Put on your glasses. Put on your glasses and you'll see me.

MAMI   *No, Leo. No hay nada mas que ver.*

LEO   There is nothing left to see?

> *He covers his eyes with his hands. Backyard games.*

RODRIGO   Count out loud!

LEO   Ten, nine... eight... seven... six... five... four, three, two... and... one... ready or not here I—

> *Lights flash bright. To the audience.*

I see them behind the hedge, crouching on the dirt and stone pathway leading to the backyard. It is a good hiding place. Not the best, but good. They don't see me. They are pink cheeked, shining eyes, innocent and perfect. Their fingers are interlaced, her foot gently over crosses his. He leans toward her and kisses her softly on the top of her head. She smiles.

ISOLDA   Leo! He found us! Look, Rodrigo!

RODRIGO   Not bad, Leo. Good time.

LEO   Thanks.

RODRIGO Um... I have to tell you, Leo, that... Isolda and I are engaged to get married.

> *Beat.*

LEO You're eleven.

RODRIGO I like to plan ahead.

ISOLDA I'm sure you'll find someone.

LEO Doubt it.

RODRIGO Leo.

> *To the audience.*

LEO Triangles fascinate me beyond any other shape— forever reminding me that not one exists, real or imagined, that is free from sharp corners.

> *A school bell rings. ISOLDA and RODRIGO sit in the audience. LEO pulls a map of the Bermuda Triangle down from the ceiling. He holds a ruler and points to the map. He speaks as though the audience is a classroom.*

The Bermuda Triangle—also known as the devil's triangle—is one of the greatest mysteries known to man. Coast guards and scientists claim that contradictory currents could quite possibly chew matter up until it is nothing but sand and pulp stroking the stingrays as they swim. But I believe that there is another force involved. Something other, that we, with our compasses and our well-ordered fact finders, may not be privy to. I believe it is possible that something or someone may vanish so completely that we may never have an answer to the eternal question: why?

> *ISOLDA and RODRIGO clap. LEO takes a bow. RODRIGO stands to be next to him.*

RODRIGO That was good. Your language. It's very... mature.

LEO I'm fourteen.

RODRIGO	You should be a poet.
LEO	Why?
RODRIGO	You suck at soccer.
LEO	Thank you.
ISOLDA	Hey, Leo. Write your poems with this.

She pulls a pen out of her pocket. LEO admires it.

A state of the art black pen with gold detailing.

LEO	That's nice.
ISOLDA	And for only fifteen pesos it can be yours.
RODRIGO	Where did you get that?
ISOLDA	From my supplier.
LEO	I'll give you ten pesos.
ISOLDA	Twelve.
RODRIGO	It's a stolen pen.
ISOLDA	I don't steal! This is business!
RODRIGO	Your little sister's toys, your father's cuff links, your mother's nail polish, your nana's candy…
ISOLDA	My father says it's just a phase.
RODRIGO	You traded your family's nana to some grandfather for a set of false teeth!
ISOLDA	So I went too far!
RODRIGO	Look over there.
ISOLDA	No.
RODRIGO	My father always says "You are not a horse—"
ISOLDA & LEO	"Refuse to wear blinders."
RODRIGO	There is a boy younger than you walking through traffic selling bananas. Do you see him?

ISOLDA *Si.*

RODRIGO Because I love you, I remind you that we are so lucky. Think about it.

> *He takes her stolen pen and exits. Pause.*

ISOLDA Are you thinking about it?

LEO Yeah. Are you?

ISOLDA Did you know that poverty is the number one cause of death in Chile?

LEO No. Where did you hear that?

ISOLDA I don't remember.

LEO I've never heard that.

ISOLDA The poverty is bad, Leo. Very, very bad.

LEO Yeah, but who said that "Poverty is the number one cause of death in Chile?"

ISOLDA Don't interrogate me.

LEO Did you make that up?

ISOLDA It's not making it up if it sounds very, very true.

LEO It doesn't sound "very, very true." You don't die from poverty, you die from poverty-related illnesses—starvation or infection—you don't just die from poverty.

ISOLDA I think a lot of people in Chile are dying from poverty related illnesses, Leo.

LEO Yeah, probably. I'm hungry. Are you hungry?

ISOLDA Want me to steal a can of condensed milk and we can eat the whole thing?

LEO You shouldn't steal.

ISOLDA And my father shouldn't sleep with the Nana so…

LEO So?

ISOLDA	So… I can do what I want. You can too, on account of your dad dying.
LEO	He disappeared.
ISOLDA	Right.
LEO	Disappearing and dying are not the same.
ISOLDA	Don't get upset.

To the audience. Netherworld.

LEO I will not get upset. I will breathe slow and long so a volcano doesn't erupt in my chest. I will not care that my mother doesn't see into my eyes ever, ever again that minnows know my father better than me, that the two people I need most would happily have each other without me, I'll shut my eyes and make love to the darkness. Can you see me now? No. Nobody can. Not when I've dropped twelve thousand houses to the earth's core and blue flames bite my breath.

RODRIGO If it isn't published poet, Leonardo Mella.

RODRIGO is holding a thin newspaper.

LEO Where did you get that?

RODRIGO Hot off the press, first edition, page 2…. Ah… Leonardo Mella is sixteen years old and in his third year here. This is the first time his poetry has been in our publication, we hope it won't be the last.

LEO It's just the school newspaper.

RODRIGO Just the school newspaper! It is a fine periodical published by the faculty and contributed to by genius students. "Unnamed Corners." By Leonardo Mella.

LEO No. Don't.

RODRIGO clears his throat. LEO looks down, ashamed.

RODRIGO   There is the sofa you sat on
Blue.
The right arm, stained with sun,
where the window licked it,
holds the seashell ashtray, balanced
On its thumb
In seven years
We have not moved it
We will not move it
Your slippers; abandoned rabbits,
nuzzling the foot of your bed
yearn for your toes to enter
and fill the empty hole
You left
In every fry pan, shoelace, tea cup
Remnants of
You
Gasping for air
In warring waters
In unknown depths
At the base of my skull
In the catch of my throat
I don't breathe
Anymore
But in the safety of corners
The unnamed corners
Between the sink and the fridge
The door and the wall
The bed and the sill...
Where you never lived
I live
Without you

   Beat. RODRIGO looks up.

You have a gift.

LEO   I have a pen. Give that to me.

RODRIGO   I will not. I'm saving it. I'm framing it and putting it on my wall. A Neruda in our midst. I'm getting you a hat.

LEO   It will take centuries for any poet in Chile to even peek at Neruda's talent—give me that.

RODRIGO   When I become President of Chile will you write my speeches?

LEO   Only if I agree with your politics.

RODRIGO   You inspire me.

LEO   Stop.

RODRIGO   You do. I mean, here we are in La Reina, this little family barrio in Santiago, like we've been all these years, sheltered. You write a poem. It's just a poem. But it's beautiful. It is. And it's just a beginning. That's what I think. But with that one little beginning I can see the world, like, opening into all these other worlds outside of what we've known here and it's like…

LEO   What.

RODRIGO   Here you are in a sweater-vest. You know.

LEO   My mother made it.

RODRIGO   It's very nice.

LEO   Thank you.

RODRIGO   But under that sweater vest. It's… like we're living these superficial lives on the periphery and all that time there's this exploding fire living underneath and we don't even notice.

LEO   There is a fire.

RODRIGO   You write from there. Your poem. It reminds me there's something underneath… there's an awareness… of humanity—like you've connected to a truth in you and that becomes…

LEO   Go on.

RODRIGO   If you tell the truth about how things really are—if everyone does, not just poets—change happens. Is your mother voting?

LEO   I. Think. So.

RODRIGO   Is she voting for Allende?

LEO   I. Don't. Know.

RODRIGO   Well, tell her. We have a great shot at this. Imagine it. Our copper will belong to us. Our miners will be treated with dignity. We will no longer be stepped on by imperialistic opportunists.

LEO   I thought we were talking about my poem.

RODRIGO   We are. It's the same thing, really. A revolution of the mind is a revolution of the people. In your words is the ache of humanity—albeit personal— but there is the need for resolution and freedom from pain and it's true, right? Honest. Your words and Pablo Neruda and Gabriela Mistral—the songs of Violeta Parra and Victor Jara... our passion—we are a country to be reckoned with, not just some third world strip of land to be owned and run by the United States of taking over everything. Think of it, Leo, if Salvador Allende is elected, in three days from now our little country will be free.

ISOLDA   Are you ready to free your minds?

Late afternoon light.

LEO   All the great poets are stoned on something.

RODRIGO   And then they die.

LEO   Everyone dies.

RODRIGO   Some sooner than others. Soli... I don't think this is a good idea.

LEO   But, it's a free country.

RODRIGO   It's true.

ISOLDA   Allende is president.

RODRIGO   The beginning of a new world.

ISOLDA   We have to celebrate, don't we…?

RODRIGO   Go ahead, Soli, light it.

ISOLDA   Yes.

> *She lights the marijuana cigarette. They are walking.*

LEO   Do you feel anything?

ISOLDA   I haven't even inhaled yet.

LEO   Now?

ISOLDA   Okay. A little.

LEO   Give me some.

> *He inhales.*

Oh yeah, I love this. Rodrigo, take…

> *He hands the joint to RODRIGO. RODRIGO inhales.*

ISOLDA   Do you like it?

RODRIGO   Interesting.

ISOLDA   He likes it.

RODRIGO   Not necessarily.

ISOLDA   Save some for us.

RODRIGO   Thanks for the experience.

LEO   How do you feel?!

RODRIGO   Exactly the same.

ISOLDA   You had tons!

RODRIGO   It appears that I am immune to intoxification.

> *They stop walking. Laugh. Look around.*

ISOLDA   Oh… the mountains—let's go to the mountains…

She takes RODRIGO's hand.

RODRIGO So so beautiful…

LEO I will write "Ode to the Andes!"

ISOLDA Thank God.

RODRIGO Isolda!

ISOLDA Uh?

RODRIGO You're so soft!

ISOLDA What do you mean?

RODRIGO You're like an animal… or a peach. Isn't she soft, Leo?

ISOLDA Let me feel.

She touches her own arm.

It's true. I'm very soft. Mmm. Can you see my veins? Is my skin thin? Look how thin my skin is.

She holds up her wrists.

What does that mean? Am I? Is thin skin on the outside thin skin on the inside? Who knows these things?

RODRIGO Um…

LEO Let's go in there.

RODRIGO The supermarket?

ISOLDA It really is such a beautiful supermarket.

LEO We should get a bottle of red wine.

ISOLDA Mmm…

LEO Some cheese. Empanadas.

ISOLDA Yes.

LEO *Leche condensada…*

ISOLDA One can. Three spoons.

LEO   Do you have money?

She takes her hand and spreads her fingers.

ISOLDA   Fingers.

RODRIGO takes her hand back.

RODRIGO   I love your fingers. They're so small.

ISOLDA   Watch. If you hold my hand up in the light, can you see through it?

LEO   Soli. One can, three spoons.

ISOLDA   Yeah, I'm going into the supermarket.

RODRIGO   Soon everyone will go to the supermarket!

LEO   That'll be fun.

RODRIGO   Soon every kid will go to school!

ISOLDA   Am I see-through?

RODRIGO   Medicine. Clean water. It's so basic. Basic human kindness.

ISOLDA   Did you know that when you touch a frog its whole body feels like it's being cut with razor blades?

LEO   The supermarket!

RODRIGO   Do we seem capable of being in a supermarket?

ISOLDA   Their skin is that sensitive.

RODRIGO   Soli.

ISOLDA   Yes.

RODRIGO   Until now, the Chilean government has been… not human?

ISOLDA   Inhuman?

RODRIGO   Yes! Inhuman.

ISOLDA   Wow.

RODRIGO   Exactly. What do you think, Leo?

LEO   I think what you think.

RODRIGO   Yes. The people united can never be defeated. We are Chile. *Venceremos, venceremos—*

ISOLDA   *La Unidad Popular al poder.*

LEO   Do you think I could climb that tree?

RODRIGO   You're Chilean, you can do anything!

>*LEO and ISOLDA laugh.*

ISOLDA   Will it always be this good?

RODRIGO   Right here it will.

>*To the audience.*

LEO   This is the moment in time. Before consequences, before guilt, before the spine begins to curve down, shorter, inch by inch, every day, til death eats the bone. Before the reality of regret, missed opportunities, stifled talent and squandered love cast every day break a different shade of sad. This is youth. Anything is possible.

RODRIGO   Ever the poet.

LEO   How long have you been standing there?

RODRIGO   Long enough.

>*Pause. To the audience.*

LEO   So I'm there, standing. And he's there, standing, looking at me. Just looking. The thing about Rodrigo, the winning thing. Is his ability to be solid and vacant in the same breath. But when he looks at you, just looks, I am special. And then I remember, no I'm not. *(to RODRIGO)* You just gonna stand there staring at me?

RODRIGO   I make you uncomfortable?

LEO   No, you don't make me uncomfortable.

RODRIGO Men who don't like to be looked at frequently have something to hide.

LEO What you see is what you get.

RODRIGO I brought you this.

> *He tosses him a hat.*

LEO Thanks.

RODRIGO There's this march all the way to the presidential palace… for Popular Unity… for solidarity…

LEO Sounds life changing but I'm not much of a marcher.

RODRIGO No?

LEO No.

> *He puts on the hat.*

RODRIGO What are you then?

> *Beat. They look at each other.*

ISOLDA I think you're a hat person.

> *Lights shift. RODRIGO is gone.*

LEO I think so too.

ISOLDA This one is so Nerudaesque.

LEO It is. I love that. Not that I'm imitating.

ISOLDA Of course not.

LEO Could I do a cowboy hat?

ISOLDA Fun.

LEO Sombrero?

ISOLDA Yuck…. Bolero!

LEO Yes.

ISOLDA My dad has one, I'll take it for you.

He looks at her.

LEO   Thanks…. You should wear your hair down.

ISOLDA   You think so?

LEO   Try it.

She unpins her hair.

Yes. Beautiful, older, sensual…

ISOLDA   Wow.

LEO   Exactly.

ISOLDA   I wish it were longer.

LEO   It's nice like this.

Beat.

Put this on.

He throws her his scarf. She wraps it around herself.

Very European.

Admiring herself.

ISOLDA   Ooh… Rodrigo would die if he heard this conversation.

LEO   "Insignificant and banal!"

ISOLDA   It is.

LEO   Not everything can be all important all the time.

ISOLDA   It can't… and this is important in a way—hats, hair…

LEO   In the world there are hats and there is hair.

ISOLDA   It's true!

LEO   And wars.

ISOLDA   And shoes.

LEO   Cafés in Paris.

ISOLDA	All of it.
LEO	We have to live in the world.

RODRIGO sees them. They don't see him.

ISOLDA	I mean... lipstick.
LEO	Yes. Lipstick.

Their eyes meet. ISOLDA holds her breath. Turns away. Looks up to the sky.

ISOLDA	Look, it's the cross of the south. It's so bright tonight.
LEO	Beautiful enough to make you believe in Jesus.
ISOLDA	Do you not believe in Jesus?
LEO	I believe, he was unjustly nailed to a cross. I don't believe in Jesus as God. But having a star-clustered cross hanging in our sky to remind us of the cruelty of man I believe in.
ISOLDA	That's beautiful.

RODRIGO enters.

RODRIGO	It is. Isolda, you are my cross.
ISOLDA	What, like your cross to bear?
RODRIGO	No, like my religion. You keep me pure.
ISOLDA	Well then call me your religion, not your cross. Religion is romantic, cross is... cross. And we needn't be so pure you know, not all the time anyhow.
RODRIGO	I know.
ISOLDA	Do you?
RODRIGO	Shh... enjoy the stars.
ISOLDA	I'm just saying...
RODRIGO	I know what you're saying.

> *He kisses her cheek.*

LEO   What is pure?

RODRIGO   Good.

LEO   Pure evil is good?

RODRIGO   You know what I mean.

LEO   What you mean is inaccurate. Purity can't be qualified. It just is.

RODRIGO   That's one way to look at it.

LEO   With words there is only one way. You either accept the definition or you don't. Pure is unadulterated. It can't be "good or bad."

RODRIGO   Okay then.

LEO   So conforming to an ideal because you believe it to be good when your instinct tells you opposite would be impure.... Don't you agree...? Soli...?

RODRIGO   Not all instincts are good so no I do not agree.

LEO   Who said anything about good? I'm talking pure.

RODRIGO   Then I would rather be good than pure.

LEO   Really?

RODRIGO   Wouldn't you?

LEO   No, I wouldn't.

RODRIGO   You always want to play the bad guy but you're not, you know—

LEO   —I know.

RODRIGO   *(to ISOLDA)* Come here, Soli.

> *He turns her face to his and kisses her gently on the cheek. She kisses him back. He looks to LEO. She wraps her arms around his neck. It is slightly awkward but sweet.*

LEO	I'm. I'm still here!
	Haze of the triangle squishes them in until it is only LEO.
	Waves tongue my skin until I am the water. The wet. The salt. Hold shrieking organs in quivering skin. I would open my mouth and swallow you whole. Break your hips cause you asked me. It is too hard to live without complete obliteration so take me. Behind the door. The sea crashing through your pelvis. Smash me inside out. Teeth, tongue, take me. Under the moon. In the dark. If I'm wanted, taken, broken. Then I exist. If I'm destroyed. I exist.
ISOLDA	Where are you?
LEO	Isolda.
	He puts his hand on her lower back to walk with her. Early evening.
ISOLDA	I was looking for Rodrigo. He's meeting me.
LEO	He told me to tell you, he can't. He's really sorry.
ISOLDA	Oh. Okay. I guess I'll…
LEO	Stay. Walk with me.
	She smiles.
ISOLDA	Sure.
	He takes her hand. Holds it.
LEO	Your hands are so small.
ISOLDA	*Si.*
	She draws her hand away gently. He looks at her.
LEO	Is he as "pure" as he says he is?
ISOLDA	What.
LEO	Is he?

ISOLDA	Is he what?
LEO	Is he?
ISOLDA	Yes.
LEO	Are you?
ISOLDA	Am I what?
LEO	Are you?
ISOLDA	I'm... I'm...
LEO	I thought so.
ISOLDA	Don't.
LEO	And that makes you happy?
ISOLDA	It's people like Rodrigo who make a difference in the world. It's people like Rodrigo who take care of the people who can't take care of themselves.
LEO	Like he does for you? You don't need him to take care of you, Soli. You can take care of yourself.

Beat.

ISOLDA	Everybody needs somebody.
LEO	Want and need are very different.
ISOLDA	...It's so green suddenly.
LEO	Spring.
ISOLDA	I looked outside my bedroom window yesterday and just like that there were leaves. I totally missed it. The burst.
LEO	The crackling of the twigs as the buds broke the bark.
ISOLDA	...I've been too busy hating my mother, examining my pores, loving artichokes, fearing death... do you fear death?
LEO	It's moronic to fear the inevitable.

ISOLDA	It's all moronic really—what will I be, will it be good enough, endless lists, thoughts, mothers, pores, lust, marriage, God for God's sake; GOD. The only thing left to do is panic. And I do. And a million baby leaves are born outside my bedroom window while a baby dies of malnutrition five miles away but how would I know because my face is in a paper bag and I'm dying to catch my breath. Thank God for Rodrigo. Thank God there are the Rodrigo's in the world. Imagine what would happen if there was just you and me.
LEO	I do.
ISOLDA	Shh…
LEO	What makes you happy Isolda?
ISOLDA	Nothing makes me happy. I am happy. I'm a very cheerful person, Leo. See?
	She smiles.
LEO	Let's go to Vina del Mar.
ISOLDA	Now?
LEO	Now. We'll take your mother's car.
ISOLDA	I definitely do not have permission to do that.
LEO	Lie. Say you're out saving the world.
ISOLDA	My mother will say "Why don't you save your bedroom? It looks just as bad."
LEO	Don't tell her. Just steal the car. You're the queen of thieving.
ISOLDA	It's true. I am. It's my only gift.
LEO	We'll drink a bottle of cheap champagne on the beach.
ISOLDA	No champagne. I refuse to drink bubbles. One should never drink air.
LEO	Wine then.

ISOLDA   Leo.

> *They look at each other.*

LEO   I prefer the leaves falling.

ISOLDA   To growing, you mean?

LEO   Do you think the flowers mind when the bees suck their pollen?

ISOLDA   I haven't... I didn't ever think of it.

LEO   Or is it easy and soft like leaves falling... the bee comes and the flower gently gives herself up.

ISOLDA   That. I think. Because honey is so sweet.

LEO   Yes.

> *Pause.*

ISOLDA   I hate this time of day.

LEO   Between day and night?

ISOLDA   The sadness.

LEO   The evening out. The universe prepares us for a darker place.

ISOLDA   I don't like it.

LEO   It's life.

ISOLDA   Not mine.

LEO   You'd rather watch your life happen from inside your bedroom window.

ISOLDA   No.

LEO   No?

ISOLDA   I wouldn't.

> *He begins to unwind her scarf (the one he gave her in a previous scene) so he can undo her blouse. They are practically touching.*

LEO   Prove it.

ISOLDA   Rodrigo—

LEO   Believes we should share the wealth.

ISOLDA   We shouldn't...

Sounds of a political rally. RODRIGO speaks as though at a podium.

RODRIGO Men shouldn't sleep with sheep but they still do it!

ISOLDA   *(to herself)* Ugh.

RODRIGO There are a lot of things in this world that we know we shouldn't do. Killing, thieving, committing adultery...

ISOLDA   *(to LEO)* What exactly constitutes adultery?

RODRIGO ...and I know that hoping for a world without violence or crime is unrealistic. But a world where we feel the weight of a child starving in our streets as deeply as if we'd lodged a bullet in her temple... that I can hope for. A man can fuck a sheep but he'd better hate himself hard in the morning.

Sounds of cheering.

This is the best country in the world! We are the first to ever democratically elect a socialist president. We are a shining example of what is possible when people come before profits, when peace comes before power. Some call us the beautiful dreamers. I call us courageous! And all of us gathered here, a youth group like no other, we cannot help but be filled with Salvador Allende's words "To be young and not to be revolutionary is a contradiction in terms!"

More cheering.

ISOLDA   He's amazing.

LEO   Isn't he?

> *RODRIGO walks over to them. ISOLDA goes to kiss him—he turns his mouth so she gets his cheek.*

RODRIGO We're going to rebuild the slum houses that were destroyed by the rain storm. Are you coming?

ISOLDA Of course.

LEO The kind of work you could do forever I imagine.

RODRIGO It is meaningful.

LEO Earthquake comes, rubble all around, in come the saviours, build it up again. And everybody cries; Yay! Quiet. Quiet. Then a big storm comes, rubble all around, in come the saviours.... Yay! Quiet. Lightning strikes, rubble all around—I mean I knew life could be pointless but you make it look so beautiful, like a dog chasing its own tail.

RODRIGO Did I do something? Is there something you need to say... Leo...?

LEO No, no.

RODRIGO Is something wrong?

> *To the audience.*

LEO Wrong? Wrong... one twitch of libido and I will... I will be...?

RODRIGO Don't do that.

LEO What?

RODRIGO That thing where your eyes glaze over and you're thinking poems or whatever. It's... really.

LEO Maybe their houses were destroyed for a reason. Maybe things happen for a reason and we don't know why. Maybe some people are rich and some people are poor and that's just life and who are we to question it.

ISOLDA Leo.

RODRIGO   (*to ISOLDA*) You go ahead with everyone, I'll be there in a minute.

　　　　　She goes.

　　　　　I know what you believe in, Leo, and I know that you make the right choices so I won't bother telling you what they are because I know that you know.

LEO   I think the rain destroyed their houses because God wants them to die.

RODRIGO   No.

LEO   That's what I think.

RODRIGO   Well what you think is wrong. God is not responsible for our housing situations. That is the responsibility of the people, and if there was an equitable share of the profits that this country itself garners, human beings would never be expected to live in rusted shacks that offer no shelter from any shifts in weather whatsoever. And since you bring up God I will state simply that God gave us the ability to choose how we treat ourselves and our fellow citizens with only a simple guideline "treat thy neighbours as thyself" which turns out to be much more difficult than it looks on paper.

LEO   So you're sharing an office now?

RODRIGO   What.

LEO   You and God.

RODRIGO   Yeah, I take mornings, he takes evenings and the devil's there all night long.

LEO   You want me to think for myself, but only if I think like you.

RODRIGO   I just want you to be honest about what you really think. Think of your mother. I've seen how you care for your mother. This isn't you.

LEO	No, me is busy picking out her clothes for her, taking her on walks, reading to her, telling her what colour the yarn she's knitting with is—it's hard enough to see with your eyes open, imagine having to describe it all the time!
RODRIGO	Leo.
LEO	Go.
RODRIGO	You do. You describe. All the time. In your…
LEO	You have somewhere to be.
RODRIGO	I just want to understand you… your…?
LEO	Words imprison my emotions so they don't eat me alive.
RODRIGO	And because you help your mother… there's no room for anyone else…?
LEO	Because I don't want to. Because there's more to living a life than making sure everybody else has a good one.
RODRIGO	More what?
LEO	More, Rodrigo.
RODRIGO	More what?
LEO	I think I heard a nail breaking wood. Homes for the homeless are being erected as we speak and you're—
RODRIGO	There would be so much time for "more" if everybody did just a little bit—if everybody just thought of the consequences to people, to humanity before they—
LEO	Everybody won't.
RODRIGO	But if everybody did—
LEO	But everybody won't.
RODRIGO	We have hope.

LEO	That's all there is.
RODRIGO	Maybe you just don't get it.
LEO	Enlighten me. Why would anyone be a Marxist—
RODRIGO	—A Socialist.
	ISOLDA enters.
ISOLDA	Because my grandfather was a founding member of the Socialist party!
	Late afternoon light switch. RODRIGO is gone.
LEO	Of course. Socialism is hereditary.
ISOLDA	No. But values are.
LEO	Is this the grandfather who beats your grandmother?
ISOLDA	Not anymore.
LEO	His values took hold finally?
ISOLDA	She kicked him out finally. And now she lives with us. You're poking me, Leo.
LEO	I'm not poking you.
ISOLDA	You are. Why? Does it make you feel better to point out that I descend from a long line of...?
LEO	Socialism and you. That was the conversation. We seem unable to avoid your...
ISOLDA	So one of the founding members of the socialist party was a wife beater. Is that allowed?
LEO	I was wondering.
ISOLDA	Now look what you've done. Poked a hole right into me. Can good people be bad? Can bad people be good?—Let's have sex.
LEO	Why?
ISOLDA	You know why.

LEO	It's not a good reason.
ISOLDA	You can't just take me apart. You have to put me back together.
LEO	Put yourself together.
ISOLDA	Impossible.
LEO	There is one purpose for sex.
ISOLDA	Babies!
LEO	No! Pleasure.
ISOLDA	Pleasure me, Leo.
LEO	How do you feel?
ISOLDA	Surprisingly together, well-adjusted and at peace.
LEO	What do you want?
ISOLDA	I want you to want me.
LEO	I want you.
ISOLDA	Good.

Moving towards her.

LEO	I want you... to touch me. I want you... here. I want you... turned over... and when I have finished licking you from behind and you've moaned your last moan... I want the whole night over again... with somebody else.
ISOLDA	Leo?
LEO	*Que?*
ISOLDA	You just said Rodrigo.
LEO	No.
ISOLDA	You did. You just said Rodrigo while you were—
LEO	I didn't.
ISOLDA	I heard.

LEO	I'd know. Believe me.
	Lights to evening. ISOLDA goes. RODRIGO enters walking. LEO joins him.
RODRIGO	I believe it. It's only speculation now but so many don't support Allende especially with the nationalization of copper and… God! If only they could see… but, well, do you think it's possible? Betrayal from the inside? From those he trusts?
LEO	Anything is possible.
RODRIGO	How much higher do you want to climb?
LEO	This is good.
RODRIGO	What a view.
LEO	This is what I should be writing about.
RODRIGO	It's a beautiful city.
LEO	It's a beautiful world.
RODRIGO	For some. If they're lucky.
LEO	I know.
RODRIGO	But for some… your father was unlucky. Disappeared.
LEO	In the Bermuda Triangle. Yes.
RODRIGO	Triangles can be dangerous things.
LEO	So can politicians. Do you have a cigarette?
RODRIGO	I don't smoke.
LEO	Don't know what you're missing.
RODRIGO	Lung cancer.
LEO	Right.
RODRIGO	You and Soli…?
LEO	Is that a question?

RODRIGO   What are you doing with her?

LEO   Everything you won't.

RODRIGO   I come in peace *amigo*.

LEO   Not jealous? Not a little bit destroyed?

RODRIGO   What would that do for me?

LEO   It must be difficult. Gets everything he wants, wins every game he plays but he can't keep his girl.

RODRIGO   He could if he wanted to.

LEO   But there's something he wants more.

RODRIGO   We plan on marrying.

LEO   I plan on nothing. You never know what's just around the corner.

RODRIGO   We've planned it for years.

LEO   You must be very proud.

RODRIGO   Pride has nothing to do with it.

LEO   No?

RODRIGO   Why are you looking at me like that?

LEO   What kind of man are you?

RODRIGO   I beg your pardon?

LEO   Just thought you had bigger balls than—

RODRIGO   What? Will you insult my manhood?

LEO   What? Will you defend it?

RODRIGO   I'm getting close.

LEO   Fire away.

RODRIGO   I don't need to drop to your level.

LEO   You're not better than me.

RODRIGO   It's not a competition.

LEO	Yes it is.
RODRIGO	I should go, I have an early morning tomorrow.
LEO	Of course you do. Saving beautiful children one thatched roof at a time. Changing their painfully simple lives, no doubt.
RODRIGO	Stop it.
LEO	Make me.
RODRIGO	I have better ways to spend my energy.

> *LEO lunges at him, pushing him.*

| LEO | No, you do not! |

> *RODRIGO turns back and pushes him.*

| RODRIGO | Get off me! |

> *LEO lands on top of RODRIGO holding his arms down. Suddenly LEO leans down and kisses RODRIGO on the mouth. They stop. Quickly get up. To the audience.*

| LEO | From a distance we're ordinary. Just two young men walking home from the park. I walk into my house. My mother sits by the radio knitting a scarf identical to the one I lost in the park in the rain with Isolda. The radio is on and Salvador Allende fills the airwaves. I am politically passionless but even still I am not immune to the call of his voice. It sounds like Rodrigo. |

> *Lights shift, LEO and ISOLDA are watching RODRIGO speak at a public rally for youth. They are applauding.*

ISOLDA	He's always been a good speaker.
LEO	Yes.
ISOLDA	Like he was chosen. By God. God said "You, Rodrigo, speak well and save the world."
LEO	He does inspire one to be good.

ISOLDA	It's luck. Being chosen. Knowing, without a doubt, what you're meant to be doing with your life.
LEO	Luck or drive?
ISOLDA	Luck. You have no drive but you were born to be a poet so you just know. There's no doubt. Are your hands sore?
LEO	A little.
ISOLDA	But if everyone was born to do something great, who would work in the factories washing toilets?

RODRIGO enters behind them.

RODRIGO	This is a great party.
LEO	What are you talking about? There's no food, wine—
RODRIGO	I meant the party. The political—
LEO	Oh yes, of course.
ISOLDA	My hands hurt.
RODRIGO	Let me see them. Mmm… you put a lot of strain on them today…
ISOLDA	Yes.
RODRIGO	Well… a builder you're not.
ISOLDA	Check.
RODRIGO	Excuse me?
ISOLDA	Just crossing another one off the list.
LEO	Isolda counts herself among the unlucky. Her profession was not chosen for her by God.
RODRIGO	Isolda, you could be anything.
ISOLDA	The woman behind the man.
RODRIGO	That's up to you.
LEO	What are we doing now?

ISOLDA & RODRIGO	Anything you want.

To the audience.

LEO   Santiago de Chile—I am everything to everyone and everyone wants something. They move and I follow. They open and I enter. Hushed in the protective and unshakeable shadow of Los Andes I am complete— where there are mountains there is the illusion of safety...

LEO moves to sit beside RODRIGO. Lights to night. ISOLDA is gone.

RODRIGO   Not so close.

LEO   There's no one around.

RODRIGO   Just in case.

LEO   Fine.

RODRIGO   It's dangerous.

LEO   I know it is.

RODRIGO   Dangerous.

LEO   I know.

RODRIGO   If anyone ever knew...

LEO   They won't.

RODRIGO   They can't.

LEO   It's you and me... it's the same as before. We're friends... talking. It doesn't look... different.

RODRIGO   I've always been "different." Somehow. My parents call me an original. When other kids were just playing I was discovering the origins of the game and why we loved to play it. What is the reason? Why? I had to know. I have to know. "You are not a horse," my father always says, "refuse to wear blinders." Give me a problem and I will come up with the best possible solution, based on facts, always on facts and on history—because only when you know that which came before and only when you embrace your limitations can you possibly hope to make effective decisions that will enable you to become closer to the idea of perfection that will save you from the—GOD! I'm an essay of myself. I can't just—I have no solution for me—I don't know... every year I grow up a little more "different." If my parents knew, you think they'd still call me an original? And smile when they said it?

LEO They don't have to know.

RODRIGO No.

LEO Nobody has to know anything.

RODRIGO Can you keep a secret?

> *They move in close to each other. To the audience.*

LEO We bury our secrets in the ground. They intermingle with the dirt and soil, the stones and worms. They drink the rain and grow like roots and split the earth.

> *Late afternoon light. ISOLDA enters. RODRIGO is gone.*

ISOLDA Everything's changing. Can you feel it?

LEO Everything always changes.

ISOLDA I don't like it.

LEO You hope for political and social change. Your life revolves around change.

ISOLDA My life revolves around hope. Hope and change are very different.

LEO So you hope for change and then hate it when it comes—

ISOLDA You're not listening to me.

LEO So stop talking.

ISOLDA	Leo!
LEO	I'm right here! I'm here.

He puts his hand on her neck and draws her to him.

ISOLDA	Everything's fine?
LEO	Fine.

He kisses her mouth. She kisses him back then pushes him away.

ISOLDA	No. Guns, knives, Molotov cocktails... there's gonna be a civil war...
LEO	You worry too much.
ISOLDA	Do I?
LEO	You do.
ISOLDA	Mmm...

He kisses her again. Beat. She pulls back.

Rodrigo's strange lately.

LEO	What.
ISOLDA	He's "different."
LEO	I hadn't noticed.
ISOLDA	No?
LEO	Why would you think that?
ISOLDA	I don't know. Why would I?
LEO	What?
ISOLDA	Where is he anyway?
LEO	How would I know?
ISOLDA	Rodrigo!

Under duress. Out of time.

LEO	Rodrigo. Just follow them, Rodrigo. Please, *hombre*. Just follow.

Morning lights up.

RODRIGO	No, I'll be in the van with the others, you two will follow us in Soli's mom's car. Okay?
LEO	How long will it take?
RODRIGO	As long as it takes, Leo. We can't put a time limit on this kind of thing.
ISOLDA	We're building the clinic and the bridge? Shouldn't there maybe be a clinic crew and a bridge crew? Who knows how to build a bridge? It's a very complicated thing, it has to be well thought out. It would really defeat the purpose of the medical clinic if everyone died on a broken bridge on the way there.
RODRIGO	Would you like to be on the bridge crew, Soli?
ISOLDA	Me? No. I can't. I can't have that kind of responsibility. I don't know how to build a bridge.
RODRIGO	Do you imagine that I haven't properly planned for everything?
ISOLDA	I wasn't thinking about you, I was thinking about the people.
RODRIGO	I have also been thinking about the people.
ISOLDA	Well good, then the people are thought of.
LEO	I wasn't thinking of the people. At all, actually.
ISOLDA	Were you thinking of the people all night, Rodrigo? Is that what you were doing?

Beat.

When I called your house no one knew where you were.

LEO	You know what? I'd like to be on bridge crew.

RODRIGO	I was in the backyard... meditating.
ISOLDA	Meditating? You would bury me alive with beautiful lies. You will make a staggeringly impressive politician.
LEO	Are we going to do like a rope bridge? Or a really sturdy kind of solid bridge? What do the people prefer?
ISOLDA	Who were you with?
RODRIGO	I'm worried about you, Soli. You're not yourself. You're smoking too much. There are circles under your eyes... are you even eating...?
ISOLDA	I don't want to eat anymore.
RODRIGO	It's a luxury to have that option.
ISOLDA	There's no good food. Rice everyday. Chicken, sometimes I hate chicken, I've always hated chicken and now I stand in line for four hours hoping for chicken.
RODRIGO	The truckers have all been bribed so nothing makes it down here. This is how they plan to eliminate Allende. Starve the people. Make it his problem, his fault.
ISOLDA	You're so busy. You're both always so busy. Entire universes are unfolding in my heart and you're missing it.
RODRIGO	Pull yourself together. You are not the centre. More out, less in. More out, less in.
ISOLDA	More out, less in.
RODRIGO	There are bigger things at stake here, Soli.
ISOLDA	What is bigger? What's out there or what's in here?
RODRIGO	Out. **LEO** In.
RODRIGO & LEO	What?

ISOLDA   What?

RODRIGO   What's out, Isolda.

> *Under his breath.*

LEO   In.

RODRIGO   Excuse me.

LEO   It's how she feels, Rodrigo.

RODRIGO   What are you doing.

LEO   It's just—she has the right to feel the way that she does.

RODRIGO   I'm protecting her!

LEO   Is that what you're doing.

ISOLDA   What's going on?

> *Pause as RODRIGO looks at LEO.*

RODRIGO   Nothing, Soli. I'm here now.

> *He takes her hand.*

You need to open your eyes, Leo. There is life outside of this little triangle. Just because you cater to every little need, every little emotion, it doesn't mean she has to. Not everyone wants to be like you, lost in your own head.

> *Lights to triangle, almost black, hazy. RODRIGO and ISOLDA are not seen.*

LEO   I'm not! God. The certainty. The conviction. Like there was never another possibility. This is the way it is. This is the way it should be. Where am I now then? Huh? Where am I now?

RODRIGO   …You're nowhere.

LEO   Rodrigo?

RODRIGO   This isn't real.

LEO	How can it not be real if you're here.
RODRIGO	There is no here.
LEO	I'm here. I exist!
RODRIGO	You think you exist.
LEO	Then I do. If I didn't exist there would be no I to think that I exist.
RODRIGO	I can't see you.
LEO	Yeah, well I can't see you either.
RODRIGO	So then.

ISOLDA whispers.

ISOLDA	I saw you.
LEO	Isolda?
ISOLDA	I saw you.
LEO	What.

Back Out.

ISOLDA	I saw you with him.

She slaps LEO's face.

LEO	I don't know what you're talking about.
ISOLDA	How could you prey on his weakness. You're an animal.
LEO	His weakness?
ISOLDA	He has a weakness for men. It's an illness. He's sick. But you. You're just greedy and unfaithful.
LEO	I'm unfaithful? You've been engaged to him since we were eleven years old!
ISOLDA	And I'll marry him and we'll be happy and you'll die sad and alone! How could you do this to me!

ISOLDA exits.

LEO	Me. At the end of it all we always come back to me. Me needing love. Me wanting more. Me all alone. And there's nothing left. No toilet paper, no flour, no fucking food! What a great idea. Let's help the unfortunate so we all end up with nothing! Maybe I am greedy. Maybe I am unfaithful. Maybe I would like a big house with big windows and a big car. Maybe if everyone is educated enough to get a good job there won't be enough jobs. Maybe if I'd really known my father I would be a better man. Maybe—
RODRIGO	It's time to stop.
LEO	Coward.
RODRIGO	It is the brave man who sacrifices himself for others.
LEO	It is the coward who tells himself lies to soothe his empty life.
RODRIGO	I wasn't thinking. I was wrong. I just—
LEO	Took what you wanted not thinking she'd starve.
RODRIGO	This was nothing. It means nothing.
LEO	The most meaningless things often give the most pleasure.
RODRIGO	And then they end. And now there is nothing but Isolda and Chile and making a difference.
LEO	A martyr is born.
RODRIGO	Why don't you write a poem about it?
LEO	I just might.
RODRIGO	You know what your poetry lacks, Leo?
LEO	Tell me.
RODRIGO	Blood.
LEO	Once there was a cut. It was so deep and so long that it cut through the entire earth. People cried out for the pain of the injured little world. They put their lips right up to the swollen crack and sucked

out the blood in stilted, sobbing bursts. But the cut didn't heal. And rusted pennies filled the bellies of the bleeding, sucking hearts as they died one by—

RODRIGO   Stop it!

LEO   The world doesn't want someone like you leading its people into the light.

RODRIGO   What's that supposed to mean.

LEO   Was that the dream? All of Chile standing at your inauguration as you hold your lovely husband's hand? You are in the wrong world at the wrong time. You'll be lucky if they don't shoot you in the back and throw you in the sea. That was not so long ago.

RODRIGO   That's why we have to change things. For every man, woman and child, equal opportunities, no discrimination—

LEO   We don't change the world. The world changes us.

RODRIGO   That's garbage! When children starve and sell their emaciated bodies on the street for sex, someone is throwing out uneaten food! You can put it on the curb and never think of it again or you can take a hard look at yourself, Leo, and know that somewhere, someone is dying because of you. Because you didn't have the balls to say enough of this garbage.

LEO   Who are you talking to?

RODRIGO   Go ahead. Mock me. Does it make you feel better? You feel invincible, lounging in your little prison of lies?

LEO   I live a lie!?

RODRIGO   Your father died. Let's start there.

LEO   Excuse me?

RODRIGO   Cancer. He smoked too much. He was not at Che's side during any revolution. He did not escape near death on a freighter that mysteriously vanished in the Bermuda Triangle. He just died, at home, with a blackened lung.

LEO   My father! My father!

RODRIGO   What!?

LEO   My father! My father!

RODRIGO   What?

LEO gasps for air.

LEO   My father!

RODRIGO   What, Leo, what?

To the audience.

LEO   My father was an unremarkable man in every way. He did smoke too much. He also ate too much and too quickly and with his mouth horribly open. One Saturday afternoon my mother made tomato salad. I can smell red tomatoes picked from the garden, skinned and diced, interspersed with practically benign slivers of onion. I can taste the sweet tang of salt on my mother's fingers which I would lick whenever she finished mixing—always with her hands—a seasoned woman cooking is after all the secret to a flavourful meal, she would say. I can see him shovelling spoonful after spoonful of her loving mixture into his mouth like it was no more than gruel. Slurping the salted, olive oil juice while the fleshy redness mashed into his uneven teeth. Mash, smack, cluck, slurp. I couldn't lift my fork off the table. He looked at me and, with his mouth full, said "Eat, kid, you look like an orphan." "I WISH I WAS AN ORPHAN, BECAUSE YOU MUST BE THE MOST DISGUSTING FATHER IN THE WORLD."

Beat.

He swallowed, silent, unmoving. Suddenly a monstrous belch cracked out of his face and he laughed. "Careful what you wish for, kid, careful what you wish for."

Beat.

They say a cancer walked into his mouth, over his throat, grabbed hold of his left lung and ate it whole. Two days later my mother went completely blind.

MAMI   *No hay nada mas que ver!*

LEO   There is nothing left to see. No. My father was at Che Guevara's side during the Bolivian revolution. He disappeared on a freighter traversing the Bermuda Triangle. He chewed slowly and inspired many with his calm, intelligent manner. He loved me deeply. That's my story. We all need one. I mean, who the hell wants to live in this shit?

Light shift. ISOLDA smokes.

ISOLDA   I wouldn't live anywhere else. I couldn't.

LEO   India, Paris, New York... you have no desire to...?

ISOLDA   This is where I exist. In this spaghetti strand of a country, between these borders, like a picture in a frame.

LEO   Pictures are one dimensional.

ISOLDA   You used to talk nicer with me. You both did.

She lights another cigarette.

LEO   Wait—I lost that—is that my lighter?

ISOLDA   Not anymore.

LEO puts his hand on her shoulder. She shrugs it off.

Did you know that when you touch a frog its whole body feels like it's being cut with razor blades.

LEO   People die from smoking too much.

ISOLDA   Random unknown people? Or fathers?

LEO   You exist everywhere. Not just here.

ISOLDA   Yeah, well my focus on reality may not be as sharp if I'm out of frame.

A glass smashes.

MAMI   *Ay! Leo!*

LEO   Mami! My mother hasn't broken a glass since 1966. Her last smash was my father's favourite mug. She cried for four days and then began wandering the house like a mime, sensing the energy of things until finally announcing that she would never break anything in our home again. It is September 11th 1973.

Three loud shots are heard.

RODRIGO   There is more greed than love in this world!

ISOLDA   Are you sure he's dead?

RODRIGO   Give a man cake and what does he do? Asks for a glass of milk to go with it!

LEO   Shot. Just like that.

RODRIGO   I am not a horse!

ISOLDA   Just like that?

RODRIGO   My father always said "You are not a horse! Refuse to wear blinders!"

LEO   Salvador Allende Gossens. Born July 26th 1908.

ISOLDA   He was a Leo. Like me.

RODRIGO   Given the choice what did the people choose? God or a golden calf?

LEO   Salvador Allende Gossens. Died September 11th 1973.

ISOLDA   No.

RODRIGO All that glitters!

LEO His last words:

RODRIGO Long live Chile! Long live the people! Long live the workers!

LEO *Viva Chile! Viva el pueblo! Viva los trabajadores!*

Machine gun shots ring through the air.

Mami!

MAMI *Es mas facil ser ciego que vidente!*

LEO It is easier to be blind than to see. We hide behind closed doors after dark, listening to the military trucks crunching over concrete—

Grey day. Cold light.

RODRIGO Was she there?

LEO No. No one from any of her classes has seen her for four days.

RODRIGO The whole family's in a complete panic.

LEO You saw them?

RODRIGO I go every day.

LEO Why didn't you tell me? I would go with you.

RODRIGO You're free to go.

LEO I didn't want to disturb…

RODRIGO You haven't checked in once?

LEO I telephoned.

RODRIGO Their daughter is missing and you telephone?

LEO They have things on their mind…

RODRIGO Damn right they do! So you go over you hold hands, you say I'm on the lookout, if I hear anything, you bring food, news, anything, but you do not telephone! Telephone?

LEO   I thought I was doing the right thing!

RODRIGO   For who?! Scared some of the fear might rub off on you? The thought of her mother crying on your shoulder too real for you to stomach?

LEO   I just thought—

RODRIGO   Of yourself.

> *RODRIGO exits. Drowning in the triangle.*

LEO   Who else is there. In the end. When the current is dragging you down the whirlpool the whirlpool like the universe knows we're entering into a darker place like they knew this was where life was leading socialists there's nothing left you capitalistic military my feet my fingers my blood into the triangle there are three sides the devil's triangle. NO! I am not one of those meditative people who take comfort in solitude. Hit me, bleed me, fuck me, break me but don't leave me. Alone.

ISOLDA   We're leaving.

RODRIGO   You can't. Doesn't solve anything. Stay and fight. Or starve for peace or… there has to be something. Something less cowardly, less afraid.

ISOLDA   This country is not safe for us right now.

RODRIGO   "This" country? Chile. We call it Chile. It's our home.

ISOLDA   Make sure you're in by curfew. Never walk alone. Don't trust anybody.

RODRIGO   Where were you taken? You were taken, right? Right off campus?

ISOLDA   On my way to class. Nowhere is safe. Not if you supported Allende.

RODRIGO   What did they do?

ISOLDA   What is the obsession with other people's pain.

RODRIGO	I'm sorry.
ISOLDA	You should be.
RODRIGO	Isolda.
ISOLDA	Goodbye.

She goes. Night falls.

RODRIGO Come with me.

LEO speaks to the audience as he and RODRIGO lower themselves to lie down. He lies behind RODRIGO. Lights are soft and sweet.

LEO We lie in his single bed. Surrounded by books. Books everywhere. And dim lighting. He'll go blind reading like this. He breathes only to his heart, too quickly. I want to feel his pain but I feel nothing. Pictures of Salvador Allende, Pablo Neruda— I wonder if he's next—bombard me. Men with feeling. Men with purpose. Maybe his parents don't know, maybe they've decided to let it go but for the first time since I've known Rodrigo Ferro I fall asleep in his bed with my arm around him.

LEO's eyes close, he is calm and then jolted upright. His eyes open. A spotlight shines in his face.

There's a light in my eye, a yank on my wrist, a punch in my belly. And fear.

RODRIGO Leo?

LEO Shh… Rodrigo, just follow! My legs walk me out the door like they knew this was where life was leading. Into a truck, doors slam. Quiet. Bumps on tires, tires on bumps.

RODRIGO *Mierda.*

LEO Stop. Doors open, jump out, walk to building, walk to building, Rodrigo, walk to building. Rodrigo.

RODRIGO No.

LEO   Follow the leader, Rodrigo, this way. Please, *hombre.*

RODRIGO   *No Leo, no puedo.*

LEO   Some men aren't meant to follow.

> *RODRIGO is shot in the chest. Lights drop. LEO*
> *covers his eyes with his hands.*

No! No! I can't see. I can't see, Mami…

> *ISOLDA and RODRIGO throw candy down at the*
> *floor as though a pinata's been smashed. They are*
> *young as in the first scene.*

RODRIGO   Open your eyes, Leo.

ISOLDA   Yeah. Open your eyes.

> *They sing "Feliz Cumpleanos" very quietly. The lone*
> *lightbulb flicks on and LEO is dropped back into the*
> *chair. His hands lock behind him as though they are*
> *tied.*

RODRIGO
& ISOLDA   Open your eyes.

LEO   And suddenly I can see. My throat is closing, I can't
               swallow, can't make a sound…. For what?! Words?
               Socialism? Capitalism? Theories, principles,
               bullshit!!

> *He is slapped.*

If there's enough food why shouldn't we feed
everybody? I can't even see your face. Why? Why
are you doing this?

> *He sits quietly listening and very suddenly he whips*
> *his head back like he's been hit in the mouth, he*
> *speaks as though there is blood in his mouth.*

I kissed Isolda Vergara for the first time with these
lips, she bit me, not on purpose. I liked it.

> *He is hit again, this time in the left cheek.*

She caught me kissing Rodrigo Ferro with the same lips and punched me with her right hand on my left cheek. Less because he was a boy, more because he wasn't her.

He is hit again and again and again and he speaks all the while.

Until I can't feel it! Until I can't feel it! And then the hit hits and I don't care. I watch it like boxing on television. Thank god that's not me. Thank God I'm not there. But if I'm not there, where am I? Where am I? Where am I...?

Quick shift to sweet afternoon glow. ISOLDA, RODRIGO and LEO stand as though at a beach looking out on the water. They pass a joint.

ISOLDA   When I'm with you.... The way the bottoms of my feet hit the concrete... the way the air eats my breath. I'm as close as I can be to what it must feel like to really be alone.

RODRIGO   You're not alone, you're with us.

ISOLDA   I know. That's what's so beautiful about it.

LEO   Being with us makes you feel alone?

ISOLDA   In the best possible sense. Not like when I'm by myself and it feels like there's... like there's pieces missing. But I'm here completely, I'm a part of everything when I'm with you and it must be, I think, what being alone is supposed to feel like. A suspended individual in a sea of everyone.

LEO   Only when the three of us are together?

ISOLDA   Mm hmm... the truth is that alone neither of you are all that much but if you were combined you would make the perfect man.

RODRIGO   I've had that same thought.

LEO   It might not have been what she meant.

ISOLDA Will it always be this good?

RODRIGO Right here it will.

To the audience. Out of nowhere.

LEO To cease to be seen; vanish from sight. To cease to exist or be known. *Desaparecer.* Now you see me.

Blackout